# Mapping
# a City

Written by **Jen Green**

Illustrated by **Sarah Horne**

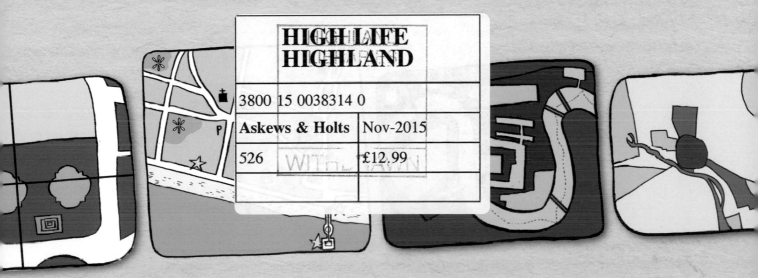

First published in 2015 by Wayland
Copyright © Wayland 2015

Wayland
338 Euston Road
London NW1 3BH

Wayland Australia
Level 17/207 Kent Street
Sydney, NSW 2000

Series editor: Victoria Brooker
Editor: Carron Brown
Designer: Krina Patel

A CIP catalogue record for this book is available
from the British Library. Dewey number: 526-dc23
ISBN: 978-0-7502-8574-2
Ebook: 978-0-7502-9117-0

Printed in China

1 3 5 7 9 10 8 6 4 2

Picture acknowledgements
Cover: top centre Shutterstock; bottom centre Skyscan.co.uk/APS (UK)
Pages: 4 Skyscan.co.uk/APS (UK); 9 left Shutterstock/Tutti Frutti; 9 right Shutterstock/JeniFoto;
11 Shutterstock; 15 Skyscan.co.uk/I Hay; 17 left REX; 17 right Shutterstock/Sergey Novikov;
19 REX/F1 Online; 21 Shutterstock/Underworld.

Wayland, part of Hachette Children's Group
and published by Hodder and Stoughton Limited
www.hachette.co.uk

# Contents

Cities and maps     4

Towns and cities     6

Sights of the city     8

A city in symbols     10

A city to different scales     12

On the street     14

Using scale in the park     16

City square in a grid     18

Directions in the city     20

Plan of a museum     22

Over the water     24

City travel     26

How land is used     28

What the words mean     30

More information     31

Index     32

# CITIES AND MAPS

Cities are places where many people live. They are larger than towns, which are larger than villages.

Do you live in a city?

This photo shows Durham, a city on a river.

Most cities are hundreds of years old. They have old buildings and also new ones, because cities are always growing and changing. There's always lots going on in a city.

# What are maps?

Maps help you to explore places such as cities. They contain lots of information about places and what goes on there. Maps show the landscape from above – like the view from a plane or hot-air balloon. This view makes it easy to find your way around a city.

**Map of the city of Durham**

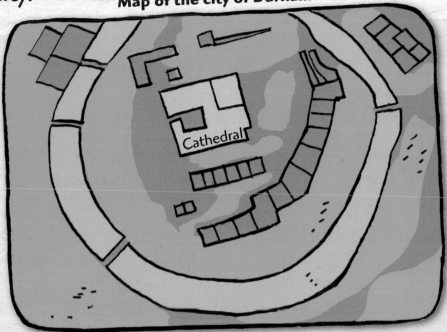

Cathedral

This map shows the same city. Many maps have a title, which explains what the map shows.

# TRY THIS!

To understand and make your own maps you have to get used to seeing things from above. Climb to the top of a tall building and draw the view below you. Don't draw cars and people – only things that are always there.

# TOWNS AND CITIES

Britain has many cities. Most cities are very large – they are home to over 100,000 people. The map below shows the UK's ten largest cities. Some are also capitals, which are the home of a country's government. The UK has four capitals because it is made up of four countries: England, Scotland, Wales and Northern Ireland.

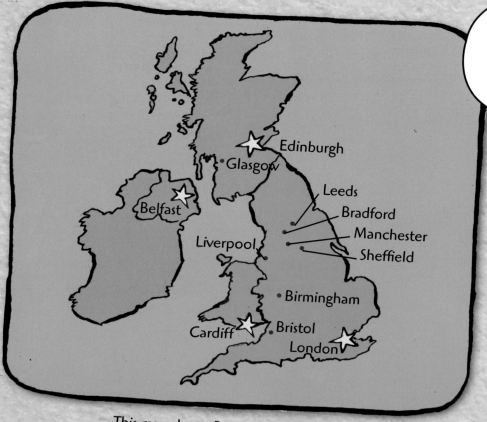

Edinburgh
Glasgow
Leeds
Bradford
Manchester
Sheffield
Belfast
Liverpool
Birmingham
Cardiff
Bristol
London

Do you know the names of the four capitals?

This map shows Britain's largest cities. Capital cities are shown with a star.

# Where people live

The UK has more than 64 million people. Most of us live in towns and cities. The map below shows where people live in the UK. Some areas have more people than others. The areas that have the most people have many towns and cities.

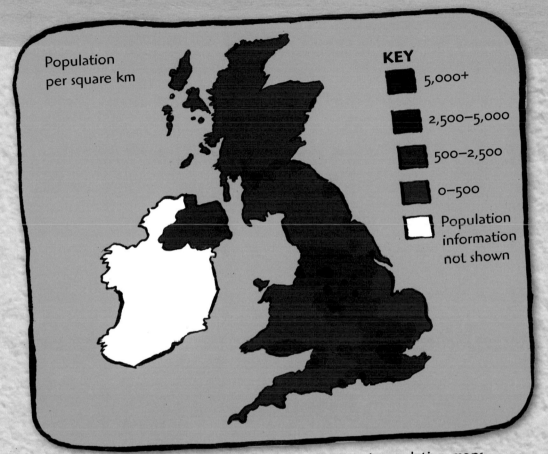

Population per square km

**KEY**

- 5,000+
- 2,500–5,000
- 500–2,500
- 0–500
- Population information not shown

Maps that show where people live are called population maps.

# TRY THIS!

Look at the map above. Which parts of the UK have most people? Which have the fewest people? Can you point to where you live? Do you live in an area with many people?

# SIGHTS OF THE CITY

Cities have lots of things to see and do. As well as amazing buildings and statues, there are shops, markets, parks and museums. Some cities have a zoo, a big swimming pool and a sports stadium.

All these places are shown on special maps called tourist maps.

This map shows the sights of Edinburgh.

# Tourist maps

Tourist maps show the famous places in a city in little pictures. The pictures make it easy to spot places on the map and also recognise them in real life. Visitors and also people living in the city use tourist maps to find their way around.

Edinburgh Castle

Palace of Holyrood

# TRY THIS!

Photocopy or trace a map of the area where you live. Draw little pictures of landmarks such as churches, shops, schools and parks. Or you could stick on little photos of these places. Are there any famous buildings on your map?

# A CITY IN SYMBOLS

Symbols take up less room than pictures, so they make the map easy to read.

Most maps don't use little pictures to show landmarks such as parks and museums. Instead, they use special signs called symbols. A little box at the side of the map explains the symbols. The box is called the key.

Brighton Centre

Brighton Pavilion

Aquarium

Palace Pier

A map of Brighton with symbols.

**KEY**

 Museum

Church

ScH School

Garden

Special sight

P Parking

## Types of symbols

There are several different types of symbols. Some symbols are coloured areas. Parks are often coloured green, lakes are blue. Other symbols are letters. A letter P stands for Parking. Coloured lines show roads and railways. Some symbols are simple pictures. A line of footprints means a walking trail.

Brighton Pavilion

# TRY THIS!

Look at the map. Imagine you are walking from the Brighton Centre to Palace Pier. Study the symbols. What landmarks would you pass on the way?

# A CITY TO DIFFERENT SCALES

Maps show areas of different sizes. They may show part of a city, a whole city or a region with many towns and cities. The size the map is drawn to is called the scale. Everything on the map is drawn to the same scale.

Everything on the map is shrunk to the same size. This is called the scale. The scale used on the map is shown in a bar at the side.

0   2.5   5   7.5   10 km

Newport

Cardiff

The map shows the area around Cardiff.

# Small and large

The maps on these pages show the city of Cardiff to different scales. This city is on the coast of Wales. The small-scale map opposite shows the whole region, but there's not much detail. The other maps below have larger scales. They show smaller areas in more detail. The larger the scale, the more detail you can see.

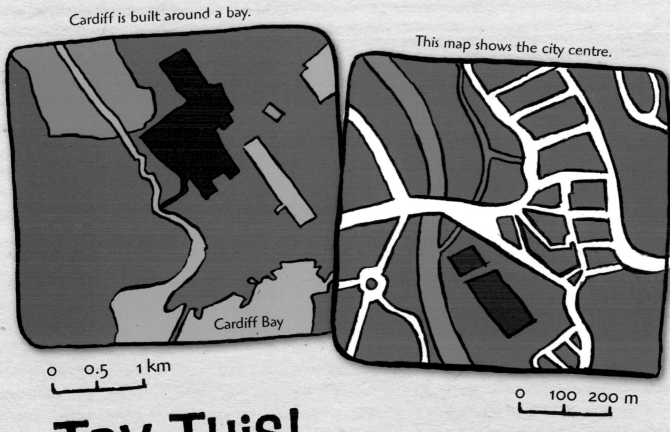

Cardiff is built around a bay.

Cardiff Bay

0    0.5    1 km

This map shows the city centre.

0    100    200 m

# TRY THIS!

Maps of different scales are useful in different ways. Look at the maps above. Which map would you use to explore the city on foot? Which would you use to reach the city by car?

# ON THE STREETS

Large-scale maps called street maps help you to explore local areas. Street names are shown on the map as well as landmarks such as parks and churches.

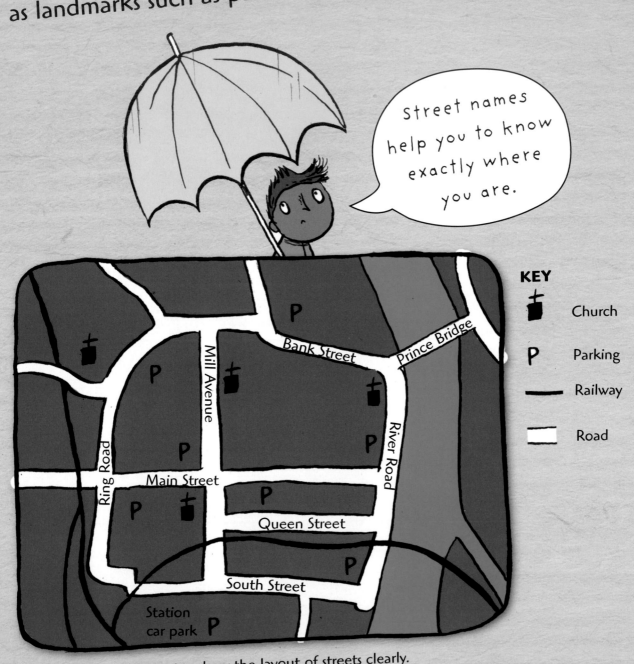

Street names help you to know exactly where you are.

**KEY**

✠ Church

P Parking

— Railway

▭ Road

Street maps show the layout of streets clearly.

## Which way?

Imagine you are standing in a city centre. Buildings on all sides stop you from seeing far in any direction. But the map shows the city from above. This viewpoint makes it easy to see which route to take to get from one place to another.

You can also see whether places are near or far away.

You can't see far in cities — buildings block the view.

Maps show things that can't always be seen from the ground.

# TRY THIS!

Maps help you plan the quickest route from one place to another. Look at the map opposite. You want to get from Station car park in the bottom left corner to Prince Bridge at top right. The map shows several ways to get there. Which do you think is the quickest way?

15

# USING SCALE IN THE PARK

Parks and green spaces are important in cities. Many city parks have gardens, a playground, a lake or a small woodland.

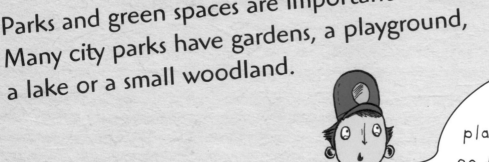

Parks are great places to play games, go for a walk or enjoy a picnic with friends.

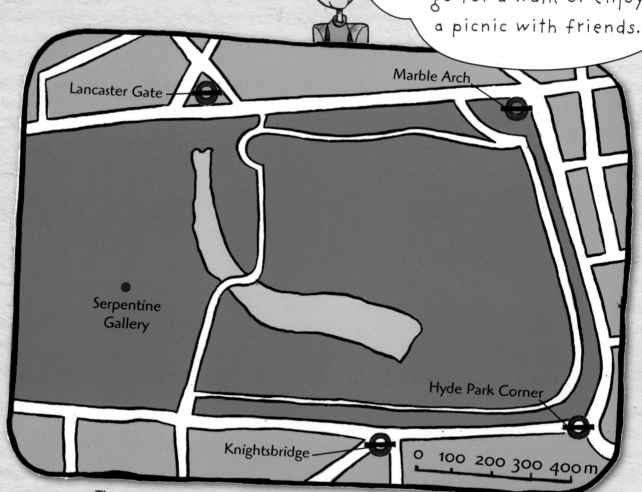

Lancaster Gate

Marble Arch

Serpentine Gallery

Hyde Park Corner

Knightsbridge

0  100  200  300  400 m

The map scale allows you to work out the distance between places. On this map, 1 centimetre stands for 100 metres.

# How far to walk?

The map below shows Hyde Park in London. This is one of London's biggest parks. The scale is shown in the scale bar. This allows you to work out the distance between places on the map. It can also help you to work out how long it would take to walk there. If you walk fast, you can cover about 3 kilometres an hour – that's one kilometre every twenty minutes.

Photo of Hyde Park

Flying a kite in a park

# TRY THIS!

Look at the map opposite. You want to walk from the Serpentine Gallery to Marble Arch tube station. Use a ruler to measure the distance on the map. Place the ruler along the scale bar to find the distance. How long do you think it will take?

# CITY SQUARE IN A GRID

Most cities have squares, which come in many shapes and sizes. Some squares are grand places with statues, others are small and leafy.

Not all squares are square — some are long and thin, round, or shaped like a banana!

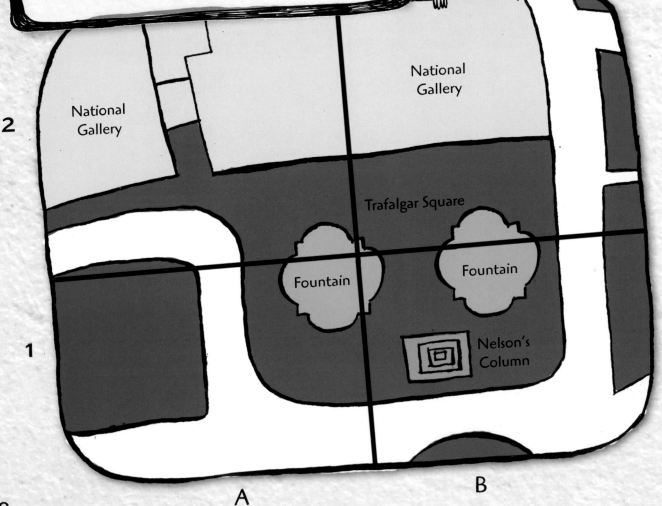

2

National Gallery

National Gallery

Trafalgar Square

Fountain

Fountain

Nelson's Column

1

A          B

# Grid of squares

The map opposite shows Trafalgar Square in London. If you look closely, you will see the map is also divided into squares. Lines running up and across the page form a grid of squares. Squares running across the page have letters, ones running up have numbers. You can use the letters and numbers to locate places on a map – this is called a grid reference.

Aerial photo of Trafalgar Square

# TRY THIS!

Grid references are always read in a certain order. You start at the bottom-left corner and run your finger along the map to read a letter. Then run your finger up the map to read a number. This gives a reference such as square B2. Now answer these questions:

- Name a feature in square B2.
- Give the grid reference for Nelson's Column.

# DIRECTIONS IN THE CITY

To find your way in a city, you need to know which way you are facing. A compass shows your direction. There are four main compass points: north, south, east and west. They are arranged in a circle.

The red needle on a compass always points to north.

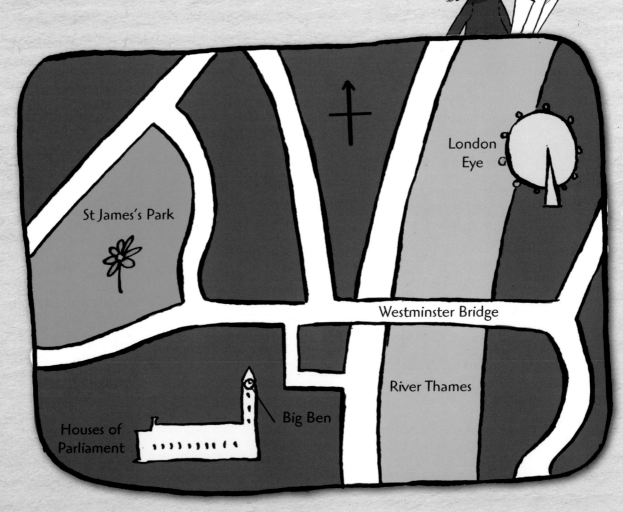

St James's Park

London Eye

Westminster Bridge

River Thames

Houses of Parliament

Big Ben

# Map and compass

Maps also show compass directions. In between the four main points are four more points: northeast, southeast, southwest and northwest. On most maps north is at the top. To find out which way to start walking, hold the map and compass in front of you. Turn around until north on the map matches the red compass needle. Then off you go!

Finding north using a compass

# TRY THIS!

Compass points can be used to locate places in relation to one another. For example, on the map opposite, the London Eye is north of Westminster Bridge. Now answer these questions.

- Big Ben lies ... of Westminster Bridge.
- What lies northwest of the Houses of Parliament?

# PLAN OF A MUSEUM

Plans are special maps that show the inside of buildings. Architects draw plans when they design buildings. Plan maps show the shape and size of rooms and features such as doors and windows.

Everything on the map is drawn to the same scale.

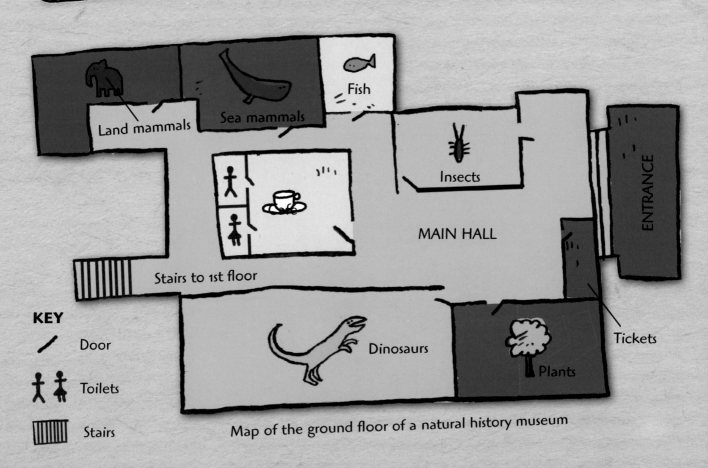

Fish

Land mammals

Sea mammals

Insects

MAIN HALL

Stairs to 1st floor

ENTRANCE

Tickets

Dinosaurs

Plants

**KEY**

/ Door

👫 Toilets

▦ Stairs

Map of the ground floor of a natural history museum

# Plan your route

Many museums provide plan maps for visitors. The plan on the opposite page shows the layout of the rooms so you can plan your route through the museum. It helps you can see everything you want to see without missing anything out.

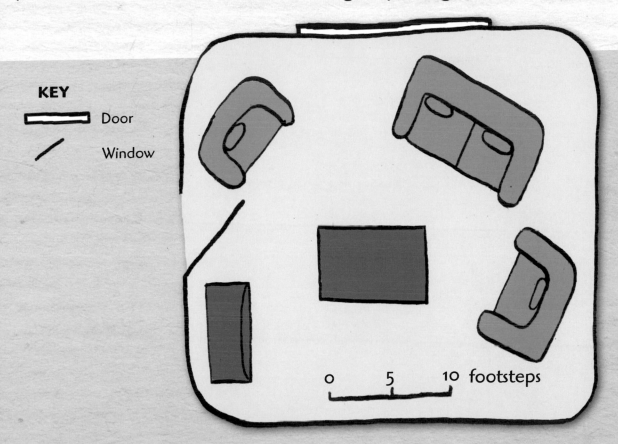

**KEY**

▭ Door

╱ Window

0   5   10 footsteps

# TRY THIS!

Make a plan of your living room. Count the number of footsteps you take to walk up and down, and across the room. Decide on a scale, such as I centimetre for each footstep. Use a ruler to draw the room outline. Now measure furniture such as chairs and tables, and add it to your plan. Don't forget the door!

# OVER THE WATER

In the UK, all cities are found near water – either a river or the coast. For hundreds of years, rivers have provided fresh water.

Rivers and the sea are useful for transport, and people also go to the seaside for their holidays.

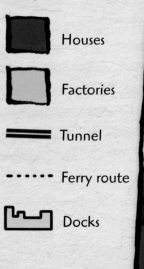

**KEY**

Houses

Factories

Tunnel

Ferry route

Docks

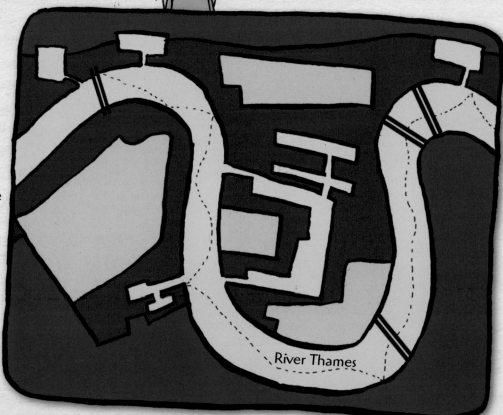

River Thames

The map above shows the Docklands area of London.

# Water symbols

Cities often grow up at crossing points on rivers. Rivers, bridges, ferries and tunnels are shown on maps in special symbols. Seaside towns and cities may have a pier, lighthouse, lookout tower or aquarium. There may be docks and ferries. All these features are shown on maps.

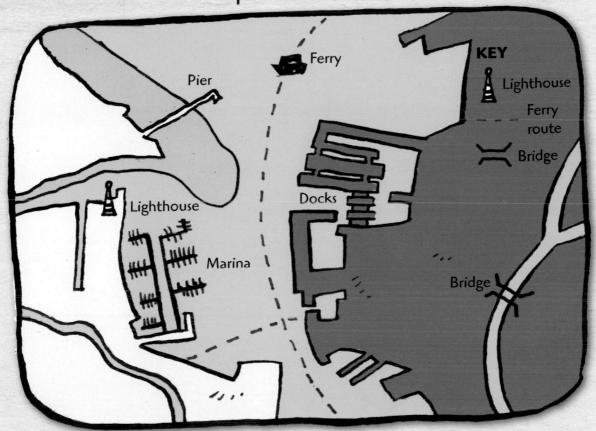

# TRY THIS!

Trace or photocopy a map of the nearest city. It could either be on a river or the coast. Colour any water blue. Add features such as bridges, tunnels or docks using the symbols shown here.

# CITY TRAVEL

Cities have many different types of transport. People go by car, bicycle or on foot. You can also take a bus, tube or train.

Map of a city centre

Transport systems such as roads, buses or trains are shown on special maps.

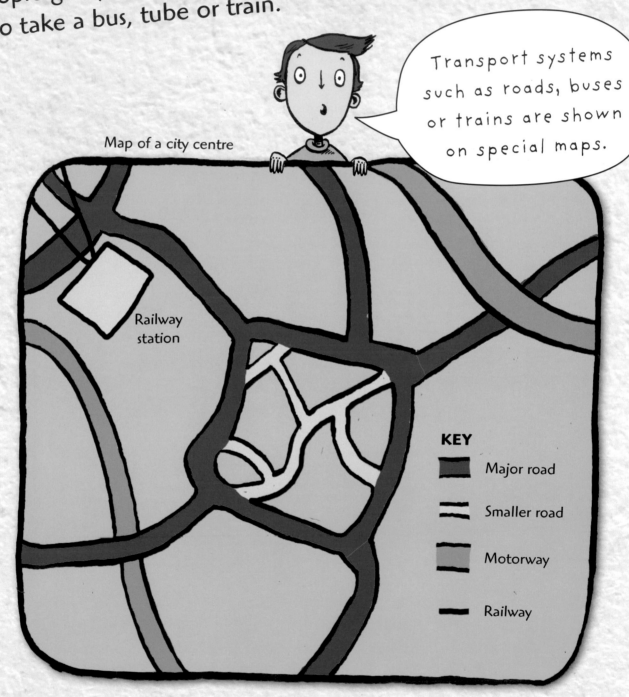

Railway station

**KEY**

— Major road

— Smaller road

— Motorway

— Railway

# Transport maps

Transport maps don't show the area in detail. Road maps just show the main roads. Bus, train and tube maps show the stops, so people know where to get on and off. Transport maps also show the connections between routes, so people travelling across the city know where to change buses, tubes or trains.

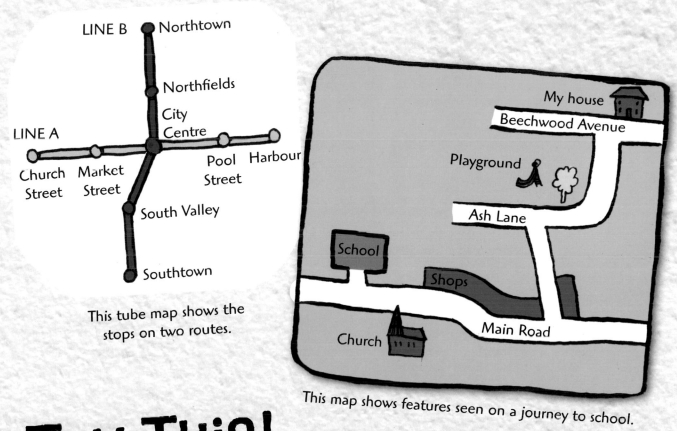

This tube map shows the stops on two routes.

This map shows features seen on a journey to school.

# TRy THiS!

Make a transport map of your journey to school. If you go by bus, tube or train, just mark the stops and any changes. If you go by car or on foot, mark main roads and landmarks, as shown in the map above.

# HOW LAND IS USED

Maps have many different uses. Special maps called land use maps show how the land is used in a city. These maps don't show details such as street names. Houses, shops, offices, factories and parks are shown in different colours. The colours make it easy to see what goes on where.

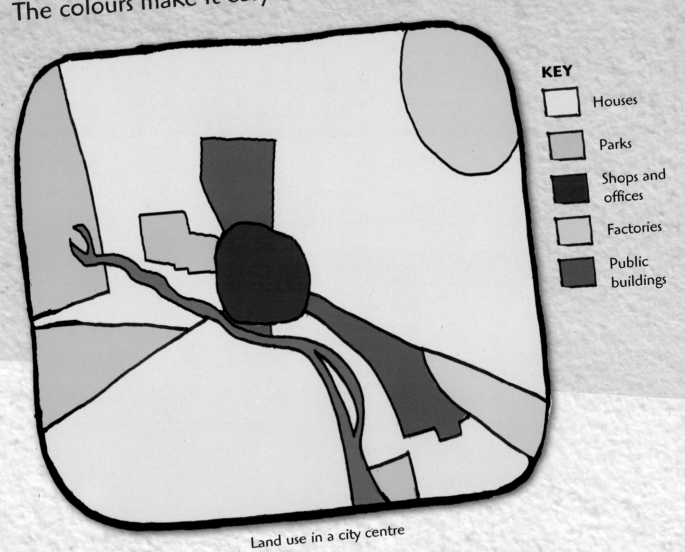

**KEY**

- Houses
- Parks
- Shops and offices
- Factories
- Public buildings

Land use in a city centre

# Changing cities

Cities never stay the same but are always changing, as new houses, roads and bridges are built. How the land is used also changes. New houses, shops and offices may be built on land once used for docks or factories.

A new map will be needed to show the changes. Maps must always be up to date!

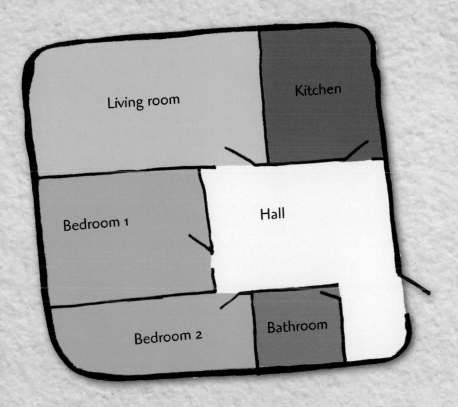

# TRY THIS!

Make a land use map of your house, like the one above. Draw the layout of the rooms. If your house has several floors, draw each floor separately. Colour all the bedrooms one colour. Then use other colours to show shared rooms such as the living room.

# What the words mean

**Accurate** Of something that is correct or right.

**Aerial view** A view from above.

**Architect** A person who designs buildings

**Compass** A tool that shows directions and helps you find your way.

**Compass rose** A symbol that shows compass directions.

**Grid** Squares on a map made by lines running up, down and across the page.

**Grid reference** Directions provided by the grid on a map.

**Land use map** A map that shows what land or buildings are used for.

**Locate** To find.

**Key** A panel on a map that shows the meaning of symbols.

**Plan** A map that shows a small area, such as a building or room.

**Road map** A map of a large area that shows roads, and is useful on journeys.

**Scale** The size a map is drawn to.

**Street map** A map of a town or village that gives the names of streets.

**Symbol** A sign or picture that stands for something in real life.

# More information

## Books

Jack Gillet and Meg Gillet, *Maps and Mapping Skills: Introducing Maps* (Wayland, 2014)

Sally Hewitt, *Project Geography: Maps* (Franklin Watts, 2013)

Claire Llewellyn, *Ways Into Geography: Using Maps* (Franklin Watts, 2012)

## Websites

### Mapskills (PowerPoint) – Think Geography

www.thinkgeography.org.uk/Year%20 8%20Geog/.../Mapskills.ppt
This site explains map skills and has lots of exercises to practise your map skills.

### Ordnance Survey: Map reading made easy

http://mapzone ordnancesurvey co.uk/ mapzone/PagesHomeworkHelp/docs/ easypeasy.pdf
Download this handy guide to map reading.

### BBC – GCSE Bitesize: Basics of mapping: 1

www.bbc.co.uk/schools/gcsebitesize/ geography/geographical_skills/maps_ rev1.shtml
A summary of map reading skills for pupils learning geography at school.

# Index

architects

capital cities 6
compass 20, 21

directions 20, 21
distance 16, 17
docks 24, 25

factories 24, 28
ferries 25

grid references 18, 19
grids 18, 19

houses 23, 24, 28, 29

key 10

land use maps 28–29
large-scale maps 13, 14

museums 8, 22, 23

parks 11, 16–17, 24, 28
plan maps 22–23
population maps 7

rivers 4, 24–25
road maps 26, 27
route planning 15

scale 12–13, 17, 23
schools 27
shops 28, 29
sights 8
small-scale maps 13
squares 18–19
street maps 14
symbols 10, 11, 25

tourist maps 8–9
transport maps 26–27
tube map 27
tunnels 24, 25

# Titles in the series:

9780750285742

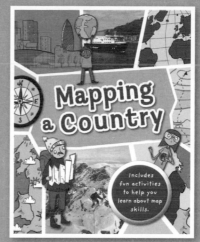

9780750285735

9780750285780

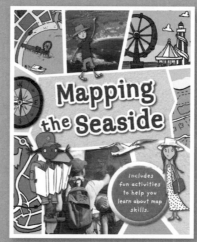

9780750285773

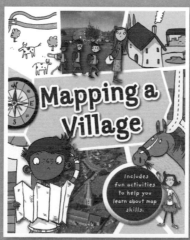

9780750285728

9780750285766